DR. BOB KENNETH

A1 Wealth Creation Codes:

Navigating the Path to Financial Prosperity

Contents

Introduction

Introduction

In the ever-evolving landscape of personal finance, the pursuit of wealth creation stands as a timeless aspiration. It's a journey marked by financial prudence, strategic investments, and a commitment to building a secure and prosperous future. In this exploration of A1 Wealth Creation Codes, we delve into the principles, strategies, and insights that illuminate the path towards financial affluence.

Understanding the Wealth Creation Spectrum

Wealth creation is not a one-size-fits-all endeavor; it's a dynamic spectrum that accommodates diverse goals, risk tolerances, and timelines. At its core, wealth creation is about harnessing your financial resources to achieve both short-term financial security and long-term prosperity. It extends beyond mere accumulation; it encompasses wise stewardship and sustainable growth.

The Foundations of Wealth Creation

Building wealth begins with a solid foundation, rooted in financial literacy and discipline. Without a clear understanding of income, expenses, and investment options, the journey becomes perilous. Thus, the first step is education—an unwavering commitment to learning the intricacies of personal finance.

Setting Clear Financial Goals

Successful wealth creation is underpinned by well-defined goals. These objectives serve as beacons, guiding your financial decisions and actions. Whether your aim is to retire comfortably, purchase a dream home, or fund your child's education, establishing clear, measurable goals is paramount.

Budgeting and Expense Management

Effective budgeting is the linchpin of wealth creation. It entails tracking income and expenses meticulously, identifying areas where savings can be realized, and adhering to a well-crafted financial plan. A disciplined approach to budgeting not only ensures that you live within your means but also frees up resources for investments and wealth-building ventures.

The Power of Saving and Investing

Saving is the cornerstone of wealth accumulation. It provides the initial capital that can be strategically deployed to generate returns. But while saving is essential, it's investing that holds the potential to accelerate wealth creation. Prudent investment choices, diversified portfolios, and a long-term perspective can yield compounding gains that substantially grow your assets over time.

Risk Management and Asset Protection

Wealth creation is not without its risks, which is why effective risk management is critical. This involves safeguarding your assets through insurance, estate planning, and legal protections. By mitigating potential pitfalls, you can preserve your wealth and secure your financial legacy.

Entrepreneurship and Business Ventures

For some, wealth creation takes the form of entrepreneurial endeavors. Starting a business or investing in entrepreneurial ventures can be a potent means of wealth generation. However, it also carries risks and requires dedication, strategic planning, and adaptability.

Real Estate as a Wealth-Building Asset

Real estate is a tangible and time-tested avenue for wealth creation. Whether through rental properties, real estate investment trusts (REITs), or property development, real estate offers opportunities for capital appreciation and recurring income.

The Role of Financial Advisors

Navigating the complex terrain of wealth creation often benefits from professional guidance. Financial advisors, with their expertise in investment strategies, risk management, and financial planning, can offer invaluable insights and tailored recommendations to align your financial goals with actionable steps.

The Psychological Dimensions of Wealth Creation

Beyond numbers and strategies, wealth creation delves into the psychological dimensions of financial success. Emotions, biases, and behavioral patterns can impact investment decisions. Emotional intelligence, discipline, and resilience are essential traits for wealth creators to weather the volatility of financial markets and maintain a long-term perspective.

A1 Wealth Creation Codes: Your Partner on the Journey

As you embark on your wealth creation journey, A1 Wealth Creation Codes is your partner and guide. We are committed to providing you with the knowledge, tools, and resources needed to navigate the intricacies of personal finance. Our mission is to empower you to make informed financial decisions, unlock your wealth potential, and chart a course toward financial prosperity.

In the chapters that follow, we explore various aspects of wealth creation in greater depth. From investment strategies and retirement planning to tax optimization and sustainable wealth management, A1 Wealth Creation Codes is your trusted source of insights and strategies for building a robust financial future.

We invite you to embark on this journey with us—a journey that transcends financial gain to encompass security, fulfillment, and the realization of your life's ambitions. Together, we'll navigate the path to financial prosperity and create a legacy that endures for generations to come. Welcome to A1 Wealth Creation—the gateway to your financial dreams.

Evaluating Your Financial Situation

Evaluating Your Financial Situation

Financial independence is a worthy goal for many people. It is the culmination of careful financial preparation, sound decision-making, and a dedication to safeguarding one's future. But, like any journey, the path to financial freedom begins with a single, critical step: knowing and assessing your existing financial condition.

In this chapter, we take the critical first step. We'll go over your income, expenses, assets, and obligations in detail. By the end of this chapter, you will have a clear and honest image of where you stand financially—a snapshot that will serve as the foundation for your journey to financial independence.

The Importance of Assessment

Before we go into the specifics of reviewing your financial condition, it's important to understand why this stage is so important. It's like starting a cross-country road journey without knowing where you're going. Similarly, obtaining financial freedom necessitates a clear awareness of where you stand financially right now. Here are a few reasons why this assessment is critical:

Clarity comes from the process of examining your financial status. It shows hidden financial patterns, uncovered expenses, and areas where you may be excelling.

Setting real financial objectives is hard unless you know where you are now. Your objectives should be adapted to your specific situation, and this assessment will assist you in doing so.

Decision-Making:
   Assessing your money allows for improved decision-making. Should you pay off a certain loan first, or should you invest? Should you limit your discretionary spending in order to save more? These decisions are based on your financial estimate.

Tracking Progress:
   As you work toward financial freedom, keep track of your accomplishments. Regular assessments will allow you to see how far you've come and change your techniques as needed.

Now, let's go into the mechanics of evaluating your financial status.

Understanding Your Income
   Income is the lifeblood of your financial universe. It is what allows you to cover your expenditures, save, invest, and ultimately generate wealth. Understanding your income entails more than just knowing your salary or hourly compensation. It is about understanding the numerous sources and subtleties of your profits.

Primary Income:

This is your major source of income, which is usually from your employment or business. Consider calculating your gross monthly income—the amount you make before taxes and deductions. This is the starting point for your financial analysis.

Do you have any secondary sources of income? This could be rental income, dividends from investments, freelance employment, or any other source. Include these in your evaluation because they add to your overall financial picture.

Irregular Income:

Some people have irregular income, such as commission-based salesmen or freelancers who make various sums each month. If this applies to you, compute an average monthly income based on your previous earnings.

Bonuses and Windfalls:

From time to time, you may receive bonuses, tax refunds, or unexpected windfalls. While they are not assured, they can have a major impact on your finances. When they occur, include them in your evaluation.

Analyzing Your Expenses

Expenses are the other side of the financial coin. They include everything you spend money on, from necessities like rent and groceries to discretionary spending like entertainment and dining out. Accurately analyzing your spending is critical for budgeting and making sound financial decisions.

Fixed expenses are regular expenses that are relatively constant month after month. They often include mortgage or rent payments, utilities, insurance fees, and loan payments. Make a list of all of your fixed expenses and their monthly amounts.

Variable Expenses:

Variable expenses might vary from month to month. They include groceries, transportation, dining out, entertainment, and other discretionary expenses. Examine your bank statements and receipts to calculate your average monthly variable expenses.

Debt Payments:

Include any outstanding debts, such as credit card bills, student loans, or a car loan, in your assessment. Take note of your minimum monthly payments as well as any additional payments you're making to help you get out of debt faster.

Savings and investments:

Don't forget to account for savings and investments. These should be classified as expenses since they represent money laid aside for future financial goals.

Irregular Expenses:

Some expenses, such as annual insurance payments or holiday gifts, do not occur every month. To account for these, divide their annual cost by 12 to find the monthly impact on your budget.

Now that you've compiled a detailed breakdown of your revenue and expenses, it's time to compute your net cash flow. Subtract your total monthly costs from your total monthly income. A positive number implies a surplus, while a negative number indicates a deficit.

Debts and Assets

Assessing your financial status entails more than just income and expenses; it also entails analyzing your assets and debts. Your assets reflect what you own, but your debts indicate what you owe. They complete the picture of your financial wellness.

Cash and Savings:

Inventory your cash and savings accounts. These are your most liquid assets, and they can be used for emergencies or investments.

Investments include equities, bonds, mutual funds, and retirement accounts such as 401(k)s or IRAs. Make a note of the current value of each investment.

Real estate:

If you own a home or other real estate, keep track of its current market worth.

Vehicles:

List the monetary value of any vehicles you own, such as cars, motorcycles, or recreational vehicles.

Personal property:

While not normally sold to fund expenses, goods such as jewelry, art, or collectibles may be valuable and can be considered assets.

Debts:

Mortgage:
If you have a mortgage on your home, keep track of the outstanding sum.

Credit Cards:
Keep track of your credit card balances and interest rates.

Student Loans:
Include any outstanding balances on student loans.

Other Loans:
Make a note of any other outstanding loans, such as auto loans or personal loans.

Other Debts:
Include any debts you owe to individuals or institutions.

After you've documented your assets and obligations, compute your net worth by subtracting your total debts from your total assets. Your net worth is an important measure of your financial health and can be used to track your progress toward financial independence.

Analyzing Your Financial Assessment

Now that you have a complete picture of your financial condition, it's time to examine what it shows. This survey isn't simply a static snapshot; it's a dynamic tool for analyzing your financial strengths and shortcomings. Here are some crucial takeaways to consider:

Monthly Cash Flow:

Is your monthly cash flow positive or negative? A positive cash flow indicates that you have money left over after covering expenses, which you might put toward savings or debt reduction. A negative cash flow may imply that you are living beyond your means.

Debt-to-income Ratio:

Determine your debt-to-income ratio by dividing your total monthly debt payments by your gross monthly income. A high ratio indicates that a large amount of your income is being used to service debt.

Do you have an emergency fund? If yes, It should cover at least three to six months' worth of living expenditures.

Consider your monthly savings and investments. Are you on track to reach your financial objectives, such as retiring or purchasing a home?

Examine your net worth. Is it favorable or negative? Strive to raise your net worth over time by paying off debts and developing your assets.

Goal Alignment:

Determine whether your financial evaluation matches with your financial goals. Are you saving enough for retirement, education, or other long-term goals?

Identify Areas for Improvement: Your assessment may suggest areas where you can improve. This could include cutting back on discretionary spending, increasing income, or devising a plan to pay off high-interest debts.

Taking Action

Assessing your financial status is more than an intellectual exercise; it is the basis upon which you will build your journey to financial independence. Now that you have a comprehensive grasp of your current financial situation, it is time to take action.

Set Financial Goals:

Based on your assessment, set clear, measurable financial goals. Whether it's paying off debt, saving for a down payment on a house, or funding your children's school, your goals should be tailored to your specific situation.

Make a Budget:

Use your assessment as the foundation for a precise budget. A budget will help you efficiently allocate your money, ensuring that you save and invest for the future while also covering your expenses.

Keep some of your money in savings. This fund will serve as a financial safety net in the event of unforeseen bills or crises.

Debt Reduction Strategy:

If your assessment indicated a significant level of debt, create a debt reduction strategy. This could include loan consolidation, negotiating reduced interest rates, or developing a debt payback strategy.

Review your savings and investing strategy. Are you taking advantage of tax-advantaged funds such as 401(k)s and IRAs? Consider automating your saves and investments to maintain consistency.

Seek Professional Advice: Depending on your financial circumstances, it may be useful to talk with a financial counselor or planner. They can give you personalized advice and assist you in developing a complete financial plan.

Regular Reviews:

Your financial examination is not a one-time event; it is an ongoing process. Set aside time on a regular basis, whether monthly or quarterly, to analyze your finances and track your progress toward your goals.

Assessing your financial condition is the foundation of your path from debt to riches, from financial instability to independence. It is the compass that will guide your financial decisions and allow you to make choices that are consistent with your goals and values.

In the next chapters, we will look at numerous tactics and techniques for achieving financial independence. From budgeting and saving to investing and long-term planning, you'll get the information and tools you need to take control of your financial destiny.

Keep in mind that your financial journey is unique, and it is molded by the decisions you make now. By taking the time to examine your financial status and create a course for development, you're already on the road to a healthier financial future. keep committed, keep focused, and let's continue this transformative adventure together.

Setting SMART Financial Goals

Setting SMART Financial Goals

We launched on a voyage of
  self-discovery in the previous chapter when we analyzed your
present financial condition. Now that you know where you
stand financially, it's time to set sail towards your ultimate
destination: financial freedom. Your financial objectives are
the compass directing us on this journey.

Goals are the lighthouses that guide you across the sea of
financial options and obstacles. However, not all objectives are
equal. Set SMART financial objectives to make your financial
path more purposeful and attainable.

What Exactly Are SMART Goals?

It's a system for turning hazy desires into concrete, actionable
plans. Let's dissect each component of SMART goals and see
how they can influence your financial freedom journey.

Your financial objectives should be specific. Vague goals such as "I want to be affluent" or "I want to save more" lack the precision required to motivate action. Instead, consider the following:

What exactly do I hope to accomplish financially?
  What makes this objective so essential to me?
  What is the purpose or goal of this goal?
  For example, if you want to retire comfortably, you can define the age at which you want to retire, the lifestyle you want to live in retirement, and the financial resources required to sustain that lifestyle.

Measurable:
  Measurability enables you to track your progress and determine when you've met your goal. Consider the following:

How will I track my progress toward this objective?

Which measures or indicators will I employ?

What is the measurable goal I want to achieve?

As an example, you may indicate that you desire to have $1 million in your retirement savings account by the time you retire. This provides you with a clear benchmark to monitor.

Achievable:

While grandiose dreams are important, your goals should still be reasonable and accessible. Setting overly ambitious goals without a clear approach might lead to frustration and failure. Consider:

Is this attainable considering my current financial situation?

What activities or actions may I take to achieve this goal?

Do I have the resources, expertise, and support I need to accomplish this goal?

For example, if you make a little wage, saving $1 million in a year may be out of reach. It may, however, be reachable over time with a well-structured savings and investment plan.

Relevance:

Your financial objectives should be in line with your values and priorities. They should be meaningful in the context of your life. Consider the following:

Is this goal important to me, or am I pursuing it because others expect me to?

What role does this objective play in my broader life plan?

Will reaching this objective provide me with happiness and fulfillment?

Consider whether your financial goals align with your long-term life vision. Setting a charitable giving goal may be appropriate if philanthropy is one of your basic values.

Time-bound:

A goal without a deadline is nothing more than a desire. Setting a deadline provides a sense of urgency and inspires action. Consider the following:

When do I want to accomplish my goal?

What is a fair timetable for completing this goal given its complexity and scope?

Is there anything I should establish as interim deadlines or milestones along the way?

Returning to the retirement objective, you may indicate that you wish to retire at the age of 65, giving your financial planning a clear finish.

Now that you've learned about the SMART framework, let's apply it to a few typical financial goals to see how it can turn them into practical plans:

Emergency Fund is the first smart code.

"I want to store money for emergencies," says the vague goal.

SMART Goal:
"I will save $833 per month from my income to develop a $10,000 emergency fund over the next 12 months." This money will serve as a safety net for unanticipated needs such as medical bills or car repairs."

The target of this SMART goal is precise (creating an emergency fund), measurable ($10,000), achievable (through a monthly savings plan), relevant (providing financial stability), and time-bound (within 12 months).

2nd Smart Code:
Debt Repayment

"I want to pay off my debts," says the vague goal.

SMART Goal:

"I will pay off my $5,000 credit card debt by making $500 monthly payments." I hope to be debt-free in 10 months, which will free up my salary for other financial goals such as home savings."

This SMART goal outlines the type of debt (credit card debt), the amount ($5,000), the repayment schedule ($500 monthly), the duration (10 months), and how it relates to future objectives (saving for a home).

Retirement Savings is the third smart code.

"I want to save for retirement," says the vague goal.

"I will contribute 15% of my monthly salary to my 401(k) retirement account," says the SMART goal. I want to have $1.5 million in retirement savings by the age of 65. This objective is consistent with my vision of a comfortable retirement."

This SMART objective specifies the commitment percentage (15%), the target amount ($1.5 million), the age at which it should be attained (65), and how it fits into the larger vision (comfortable retirement).

Why SMART Goals Are Important

Setting SMART financial objectives is important for a number of reasons:

Clarity:
SMART goals provide direction and clarity. They turn abstract goals into specific plans, making it easier to focus on what matters.

SMART goals foster a sense of purpose and motivation. They provide you a particular goal to aim toward, which may be a tremendous motivator for action.

Accountability:
Because SMART goals are clearly measurable, you can hold yourself accountable. Tracking your progress on a regular basis keeps you on target.

Prioritization:
When your goals are clear, you can prioritize your actions and resources. You know how to spend your time, money, and energy.

Adaptability:
As circumstances change, SMART goals can be altered. If unforeseen challenges or possibilities arise, you can alter your goals accordingly.

Balancing Short-Term and Long-Term Objectives

Setting SMART financial goals requires striking a balance between short-term and long-term objectives. Short-term objectives are concerned with urgent demands and near-term aspirations, whereas long-term goals define your financial destiny over time. Both are necessary components of a well-rounded financial strategy.

Short-Term Objectives

Short-term goals are typically one year or less in duration. In the near run, they meet immediate financial demands and create a sense of success. Common short-term objectives include:

Putting money aside for an emergency.
   Paying off high-interest loans.
   Putting money aside for a holiday.
   Paying for upcoming medical expenditures.
   Refilling an empty savings account.
   Short-term goals are important because they address present financial stability and provide a safety net for unanticipated needs. Achieving short-term targets also offers the drive and momentum required to tackle longer-term objectives.

Long-Term Objectives
   Long-term goals often span several years or decades and extend beyond the one-year time frame. They include key life

events as well as future goals. Long-term financial objectives include the following:

Retirement preparation.
   Putting money aside for a child's education.
   Purchasing a home.
   Investing for financial security.
   Estate planning and objectives.
   Long-term objectives necessitate a more thorough and consistent strategy. They frequently entail regular saving, investment, and strategic planning. While the effects may not be obvious right away, the financial security and independence they provide in the long run are well worth the work.

The Balancing Act
   Balancing short-term and long-term goals can be difficult, but it is an essential part of financial planning. Neglecting one in favor of the other might result in financial imbalances.

Consider the following tactics for striking the proper balance:

Set your goals in order of priority.
   Paying off high-interest debt, for example, may take precedence over saving for a vacation.

Allocate Resources:
   Set aside a percentage of your earnings for both short- and long-term goals. This assures that you are progressing on

several fronts.

revise Over Time:

Be prepared to revise your goal allocations as circumstances change. If you get a raise, think about raising your contributions to both short-term and long-term goals.

Set up automatic payments to savings and investment accounts for both short and long-term goals. Automation ensures consistency.

Review on a regular basis:

Review your goals on a regular basis to verify they are still relevant. Adjustments may be required as a result of life events such as marriage, motherhood, or work changes.

Celebrate Milestones:

Recognize your accomplishments, both big and small. Recognizing your progress on short-term goals might provide the incentive you need to stick to long-term ambitions.

Balancing short-term and long-term goals is a fluid process that changes as your life changes. The goal is to keep your eyes on both horizons, ensuring that your immediate financial demands are covered while also planning for your financial future.

Aligning Your Objectives with Your Values

While the SMART framework and the balance between short-term and long-term goals bring structure to your financial planning, there is another important factor to consider: goal alignment with values.

Your values serve as guiding factors in your life decisions. They reflect what is most important to you, what you believe in, and what gives your life meaning and purpose. When your financial goals and values are in sync, your financial journey becomes about more than simply the destination; it also becomes about the joy you get from pursuing those goals.

How to make sure your financial goals align with your values:

Identify Your basic Values: Spend some time identifying your basic values. These may include family, safety, adventure, philanthropy, personal development, or creativity.

Examine Your Financial Goals: Examine your financial goals to see if they correspond with your values. If family is a major value, your goals could include investing for your children's education or planning a family vacation.

Prioritize Your principles:

If you have competing ambitions, prioritize those that are consistent with your core principles. This guarantees that you are allocating resources to what is genuinely important to you.

Find Meaning in Your Goals:

When your goals are in line with your values, they become more than just financial targets. They transform into meaning-ful pursuits that provide happiness and contentment.

Stay Committed:

When your financial goals align with your beliefs, you're more likely to stick with it, especially when faced with obstacles or failures.

Consider the following scenario:

Two people set a $10,000 savings target for themselves. Person A's aim is motivated by a desire to travel and learn about various cultures, which is in line with their fundamental value of adventure. Person B's aim is motivated by a sense of competitiveness with their peers, which aligns with their achievement value.

Both individuals may achieve their financial goals, but Person A is more likely to feel satisfied and fulfilled by doing so because it matches with their values. Person B, on the other hand, may feel empty or unfulfilled because the aim does not align with their genuine priorities.

Aligning your financial goals with your beliefs may turn the path into a source of joy and purpose, rather than just a means to an end.

Aligning Values and Objectives

Let's look at how aligning values and goals might emerge in practice:

Family is a core value.

To match this ideal, I've set a goal of saving $5,000 for a family vacation to a location we've always wanted to visit. This goal will allow us to bond, try new things, and enhance our family ties."

In this case, the importance of family motivates the goal of saving for a vacation. The goal isn't just about the place or the money saved; it's also about the significant experiences and memories the family will share.

Setting SMART financial objectives that are in line with your beliefs is a game changer on the road to financial independence. As you traverse your financial journey, these goals provide clarity, drive, and a sense of purpose. Whether your objectives are short-term or long-term, they serve as guides for your decisions and activities.

As you set out to achieve your financial objectives, keep in mind that it's not just about getting there—it's also about the fulfillment and happiness you get from pursuing goals that correspond with your beliefs. In the next chapters, we will look at numerous techniques and tactics to assist you achieve your goals. Keep committed, keep focused, and let's continue on this path to financial independence together.

Budgeting for Financial Success

Budgeting for Financial Success

Your budget is your compass on the road to financial independence. It is the tool that assists you in navigating the frequently turbulent financial waters and steering your route toward your objectives. This chapter focuses on the art and science of budgeting, a critical ability that can mean the difference between financial success and uncertainty.

The Importance of Budgeting

Budgeting is more than just limiting your spending; it is about gaining control and making informed financial decisions. Here's why budgeting is important on the road to financial independence:

Financial Intelligence:

A budget gives you a clear picture of your income and expenses. It reveals your spending habits as well as places where you may save and invest more effectively.

Budgeting ensures that your expenditure is in line with your financial goals. It assists you in allocating resources to what is most important, whether that is paying off debt, saving for a home, or investing for retirement.

Emergency Planning:

Having a budget in place allows you to be better prepared for unforeseen spending or crises. Your budget can include provisions for creating an emergency fund.

Debt Reduction:

If you have outstanding obligations, a budget might be an effective instrument for reducing them. It enables you to set aside additional income for debt repayment.

Savings and investments:

Budgeting allows you to set money aside for savings and investments in a methodical manner. It ensures that you are always working towards your financial objectives.

Financial Discipline:

Budgeting helps to build financial discipline. It urges you to live within your means and prevent spending that is impulsive or needless.

Now, let's get into the nuts and bolts of generating and sticking to a budget.

Planning Your Budget

Budgeting is a step-by-step procedure that starts with assessing your income and expenses. Here's where to begin:

Step 1:
Compile Financial Data

Begin by gathering all essential financial data. This includes the following:

Income statements or pay stubs.
Statements from the bank.
Statements from credit cards.
Bills for utilities.
Statements of loan.
Any additional financial documents.

Step 2:
Determine Your Earnings

Total your monthly income from all sources. This could include:

Wages or salary.
Rental revenue.
Income from investments (dividends, interest, and so on).
Earning money as a side hustle or as a freelancer.
Any other sources of income.

Step 3:
Write down your expenses

Typically, expenses fall into two categories:

Fixed expenses are regular expenses that remain essentially constant month after month. Typical fixed expenses include:

Payments for rent or mortgage.

    Bills for utilities (electricity, water, and gas).

    Premiums for insurance (health, car, and house).

    Loan payments (auto loans, student loans, and so on).

    Services that require a subscription (internet, streaming, etc.).

    Variable expenses are those that change from month to month.

These are some examples:

Groceries.

    Eating out.

    Transportation expenses (gas, public transportation, etc.).

    Activities for recreation and leisure.

    Personal care and miscellaneous costs.

    Step 4: Classify and calculate

Sort your spending into categories so you can understand where your money is going. To gain a comprehensive view of your spending habits, total each category. Budget categories that are common include:

Housing.

    Transportation.

    Food.

    Repayment of debt.

    Entertainment.

    Investing and saving.

    Miscellaneous.

Step 5:

    Calculate Your Available Income

To calculate your disposable income, subtract your entire expenses from your total income. This is the amount of money you have left after paying for your essentials.

Step 6:
  Establish Financial Objectives

Consider your financial goals before finishing your budget. Trying to pay off high-interest debt? Putting money aside for an emergency? Set aside a percentage of your disposable income for these objectives.

Step 7:
  Examine and Adjust

Your initial budget is merely a starting point. It is critical to review and alter it on a regular basis to ensure that it is in line with your goals and reflects changes in your financial circumstances. Update your budget if your income or expenses change.

Budgeting Techniques
  Now that you've established a basic budget, let's look at some budgeting tactics to help you make the most of your financial resources.

1.
  The Rule of 50/30/20
  A prominent budgeting guideline is the 50/30/20 rule, which proposes dividing your after-tax income into three categories:

50% for necessities: This comprises necessities such as housing, utilities, transportation, and groceries.

30% for desires:
   This category includes non-essential expenditure on things like dining out, entertainment, and hobbies.

Set aside 20% of your salary for savings and debt repayment.

The 50/30/20 rule provides a simple framework for balancing your financial objectives.

2.
   Budgeting from zero

Zero-based budgeting is a strategy of allocating each dollar of your revenue to a specified goal. The idea is to have your revenue less your costs equal zero. This method urges you to put every dollar to work, whether it's for critical spending, debt repayment, or future savings.

3.
   Budgeting via Envelope

Envelope budgeting is a cash-based strategy in which you distribute a set amount of money to envelopes labeled with various expenditure categories (groceries, dining out, entertainment, and so on). When an envelope is empty, you are no longer able to spend in that area until the next budgeting month. This strategy is especially useful for controlling variable expenses.

4.
Budgeting Automation

Automation is an effective budgeting technique. As soon as you receive your paycheck, set up automatic transfers to your savings and investing accounts. This ensures that saving and investing take precedence over discretionary spending.

Budgeting for an Emergency Fund

Consider including a budget line item for establishing and managing your emergency fund. Small, consistent efforts might pile up over time.

Budgeting for Unexpected Expenses
Irregular expenses, such as annual insurance payments, holiday gifts, or car maintenance, can wreak havoc on your budget if not well prepared for. Here's how to deal with these costs:

Identify Irregular Expenses:
Make a list of unexpected expenses that you expect to incur throughout the year.

Calculate the Monthly Impact:
Divide the annual cost of each irregular expense by 12 to find how much you need to set away each month.

Open a second savings account or designate a portion of your existing emergency money as a sinking fund for unexpected expenses. Make a monthly contribution to this fund to pay these projected costs when they arise.

Adjust Your Budget:

Make sinking fund contributions a regular budget area to en-sure you consistently set aside money for unexpected expenses.

The Function of Emergency Funds

Budgeting and emergency funds go hand in hand. An emergency fund is a financial safety net that offers a cushion for unforeseen bills or crises. It keeps you from having to rely on credit cards or loans for unforeseen expenses.

The quantity of your emergency fund should correspond to your financial status and level of comfort. A good rule of thumb is to have three to six months' worth of necessary living expenditures in your emergency fund. This varies according to circumstances such as employment stability, family size, and personal preferences.

Ways to incorporate an emergency fund into your budget:

Set a Monthly Contribution:

Make a budget line item for contributing to your emergency fund. Set aside a percentage of your monthly disposable money to establish and manage this fund.

Automate donations:

To ensure consistency, automate your emergency fund dona-tions. Consider it a non-negotiable expense.

Use Windfalls:

Windfalls, such as tax returns or work bonuses, can help you build your emergency fund. Consider putting a percentage of your unexpected income into this fund.

Review and replenish your emergency fund on a regular basis to ensure it meets your demands. Make a plan for replenishing funds if you use them for an emergency.

Budgeting is the bedrock of good financial management. It is the instrument that enables you to take charge of your financial future, make informed decisions, and work toward your objectives. While budgeting may appear to be a restraint at first, it is a path to financial freedom and independence.

Remember that a budget is not static; it is dynamic and should change as your life circumstances change. Review and alter your budget on a regular basis to reflect changes in your income, expenses, and financial goals.

In the following chapters, we will look at debt reduction options, saving and investing for the future, and retirement planning. Your budget will be crucial in these activities, ensuring that your financial decisions are in line with your long-term goals. Stay committed, stay focused, and let's continue this revolutionary path toward financial independence together.

Debt Relief and Financial Independence

Debt Relief and Financial Independence

Debt is a strong foe on your path to financial independence. It can bind you to financial hardship, limit your options, and stymie your progress toward your objectives. In this chapter, we'll look at tactics for crushing debt and paving the route to financial freedom, rather than just managing it.

The Debt Problem

Debt is neither good nor evil in and of itself. It is a financial tool that can be utilized wisely or irresponsibly. Understanding the difference between good and bad debt and having a plan to manage and remove the latter is critical to financial success.

Bad Debt vs. Good Debt

Good debt is utilized to finance ventures that have the potential to increase in value or create revenue over time. Typical examples include:

Mortgages:

Borrowing to buy a home is commonly considered good debt because real estate tends to increase over time, and mortgage interest rates are typically lower than other types of loans.

Student Loans:

Because investing in school can lead to increased earning potential and professional prospects, many people consider student loans to be a justifiable type of debt.

Entrepreneurs can use business loans to start or develop their firms, which can result in improved income and financial security.

Low interest rates, tax incentives (such as mortgage interest deductions), and a clear route to eventual payback describe good debt.

Bad Debt:

On the other side, bad debt is utilized to finance consumer goods or expenses that do not produce long-term value or income. Typical examples include:

Credit Card Debt:

One of the most well-known types of bad debt is high-interest credit card debt. It frequently builds as a result of reckless spending or an emergency and can swiftly spiral out of hand.

Car Loans:

While owning a car is necessary, financing it with a high-interest loan can be detrimental to your financial health, particularly if you purchase a car that depreciates quickly.

Personal Loans:

Borrowing for non-essential needs such as holidays or luxury items is considered bad debt.

Bad debt often involves high interest rates, provides no tax benefits, and, if not managed effectively, can lead to a cycle of financial stress.

Making a Debt Reduction Strategy

A well-structured debt reduction plan is required to fight your debt and move toward financial independence. Here's a step-by-step tutorial for making one:

Step 1:
  Recognize Your Debt

The first step in dealing with debt is to face it head on. Collect all of your debt statements, including credit card statements, loan statements, and any other outstanding balances. Make a detailed list that includes the following information about each debt:

The whole sum owed.
  The rate of interest.
  The smallest monthly payment.
  The deadline.
  This inventory offers a clear picture of your debt situation.

Step 2:

Establish Debt Reduction Objectives

Determine your debt-reduction objectives. These objectives should be consistent with your overall financial plan and may include the following:

Paying off all high-interest credit card debt within a year.
Reducing student loan balances by a specified proportion in three years.
Within two years, I will have completely paid off my car loan.
Setting defined, quantifiable, and achievable goals provides a road map for your debt-reduction strategy.

Step 3:
Sort Through Your Debts

Prioritize your debts once you've established your debt list and goals. There are two basic approaches for prioritizing:

The avalanche technique entails paying off debts with the highest interest rates first, while making minimum payments on other bills. This method reduces the overall interest paid over time.

The snowball strategy prioritizes paying off the smallest obligations first, regardless of interest rates. This strategy delivers a psychological boost because it allows you to achieve quick victories, which might drive you to handle greater debts.

Select the technique that corresponds to your tastes and financial circumstances. Both have advantages, so choose the one that keeps you motivated.

Step 4:

Make a Debt Repayment Budget

Set aside a chunk of your budget for debt repayment. Determine how much you can easily commit to debt reduction each month. This sum should correspond to your disposable income and be in addition to the minimum payments on all debts.

Step 5:

Eliminate Unnecessary Expenses
Examine your budget for areas where you may cut costs. Consider temporarily cutting back on discretionary spending, such as dining out or entertainment, in order to devote more income to debt reduction.

Step 6:

Increase Your Earnings
Look for ways to raise your income, even if only temporarily, to help you pay off your debt faster. Side jobs, freelance employment, or selling unneeded stuff can all help you reach your debt-reduction goals.

Step 7:

Discuss Interest Rates
Inquire with your creditors about lowering interest rates, particularly on high-interest credit cards. Over time, a reduced interest rate can dramatically reduce the total cost of debt.

Step 8:

Maintain Consistency and Monitor Progress

The key to successful debt reduction is consistency. Make on-time loan payments and stick to your plan. Keep track of your progress as you pay down each bill. To keep motivated, celebrate small victories along the road.

Additional Debt-Reduction Strategies

Consider the following debt-reduction techniques in addition to the actions indicated above:

Debt Consolidation:

If you have several high-interest debts, you should look into debt consolidation options. This entails obtaining a new loan with a reduced interest rate in order to pay off old debts. Consolidation can help you simplify your debt payments while potentially lowering your interest costs.

Balance Transfer:

Some credit card companies offer balance transfer deals with low or no interest for a limited time. Transferring high-interest credit card balances to a promotional rate card can help you save money on interest and pay off debt faster.

Debt Counseling:

If you're drowning in debt and finding it difficult to manage it on your own, try obtaining help from a respected credit counseling firm. They can assist you in developing a debt management strategy and negotiating with creditors.

Bankruptcy:

While it should be considered a last resort, bankruptcy may be a possibility for those who are drowning in debt. Consult with a bankruptcy professional to see whether this is the best option for you.

The Psychological Aspects of Debt Relief

Dealing with debt is a psychological as well as a financial struggle. The worry and anxiety that debt may cause are genuine, and they can have an impact on your entire well-being. Here are some techniques for dealing with the psychological aspects of debt repayment:

Mindset Change:

Change your mindset from scarcity and fear to abundance and empowerment. Instead of focusing on what you lack, concentrate on what you can accomplish through conscientious debt reduction.

Visualization:

Imagine your life free of debt. Consider the freedom and opportunities that will become available after you are debt-free. Visualization can be a very effective motivator.

Seek Help:

Discuss your debt-reduction objectives with a trusted friend or family member who can provide support and accountability.

Celebrate Milestones:

Commemorate your accomplishments and milestones along the journey. Recognizing your accomplishments, whether it's paying off a credit card or meeting a specific debt reduction goal, can enhance your morale.

Debt reduction can be mentally and emotionally draining. To deal with stress, practice self-care. Exercise, meditation, and relaxation practices can all aid in your ability to remain focused and resilient.

The Road to Financial Independence

Keep your sights on the prize: financial freedom, as you work carefully to eradicate your debt. Consider a life without debt payments, where your income is free to be directed toward your objectives and desires.

Financial independence is more than just being debt-free; it is also about having options. It is the capacity to:

Invest and save for the future.

Donate to causes that you care about.

Retire on your own terms and schedule.

Each move you take to reduce and eliminate debt puts you closer to realizing these goals. It's a path that demands perseverance, patience, and discipline. However, the advantages are tremendous.

Debt can be a significant impediment to financial freedom, but it is not insurmountable. You can crush your debt and pave the route to financial freedom with a clear plan, drive, and consistency.

Debt removal requires a shift of your financial mentality and habits, not merely a financial exercise. As you pay off your debts, you'll gain the knowledge and strength needed to make wise financial decisions for the rest of your life.

In the next chapters, we'll look at ways for accumulating money, saving for retirement, and leaving a financial legacy. Your dedication to debt elimination is a critical step in achieving these larger financial objectives. Keep your focus and determination, and let's continue this empowering journey collectively.

Wealth Creation Strategies

Wealth Creation Strategies

Congratulations on gaining debt control and moving closer to financial freedom! Now that you've defeated the debt monster, it's time to shift your financial focus to wealth creation. In this chapter, we'll look at tactics and ideas that can help you accumulate wealth in a systematic and logical manner.

The Wealth Attitude

Wealth creation is more than simply statistics; it is also a state of mind. Your money views and attitudes have a big impact on your capacity to accumulate wealth. Here are some essential wealth mindset principles:

Long-Term Perspective:

Wealth builders are concerned with the long term. They recognize that accumulating significant money takes time and discipline. They avoid get-rich-quick scams in favor of gradual, consistent success.

Financial Education:

A wealth mindset entails ongoing education in personal finance and investing. Learn about several investing possibilities, tax methods, and financial planning.

Wealth builders establish specific financial goals. They know what they want to accomplish, whether it's retiring early, purchasing a home, or leaving a legacy. Goals provide focus and motivation.

Financial Discipline:
   Discipline is essential for wealth accumulation. It entails living within your means, saving and investing consistently, and avoiding excessive debt.

Risk Management:
   Wealth creators recognize and manage risk. They diversify their finances, save for emergencies, and insure their assets and loved ones.

Adaptability:
   As the financial world evolves, so must wealth builders. They are willing to adapt their strategies as economic conditions change or new opportunities emerge.

The Wealth-Generation Pyramid
   Consider wealth creation to be a pyramid. The fundamental ideas and practices that provide stability and support are at the foundation. As you progress up the pyramid, you will meet methods with increased risk and potentially higher profits. Let's take a look at each level of the wealth-creation pyramid:

Level 1:
   Financial Basis

Your financial foundation is located at the bottom of the pyramid. This level focuses on developing important financial habits and safeguards:

Maintain an emergency fund of three to six months' worth of living expenses. This serves as a safety net for unforeseen situations such as medical bills or job loss.

Debt Management:
Maintain and minimize any outstanding non-mortgage debt. Pay off your high-interest debt as soon as feasible.

Budgeting:
Follow your budget and keep control of your spending. Regularly review and adapt your budget to reflect changes in your financial status.

Insurance:
Make certain you have adequate insurance coverage, such as health, vehicle, house, and life insurance. Insurance shields you and your family from financial hardship.

Estate Planning:
Make or revise your will. This comprises a will, power of attorney, and healthcare directive. Estate planning guarantees that your intentions be carried , while also reducing taxes and legal expenditures.

Level 2:
Investing and Savings

49

The second level of the pyramid is concerned with saving and investing in order to increase your wealth:

Contribute as much as possible to tax-advantaged retirement plans, such as a 401(k) or IRA. These accounts provide tax advantages while compounding your savings over time.

Tax-Efficient Investing:
To reduce capital gains taxes, consider tax-efficient investment strategies such as storing investments in tax-advantaged accounts and implementing tax-loss harvesting.

Diversification:
To spread risk, diversify your investing portfolio. A well-diversified portfolio includes a variety of asset classes, including stocks, bonds, and real estate.

Regular Contributions:
Make regular contributions to your investing accounts. Saving and investing consistently is essential for long-term wealth growth.

Level 3:
Advanced Wealth Creation
At this level, you investigate more complex wealth-building tactics, such as: Real estate, which can generate income as well as prospective appreciation.

Invest in individual equities or equity mutual funds on the stock market. Investigate and select investments that are compatible with your financial objectives and risk tolerance.

Entrepreneurship:

If you have a business concept or a passion project, look into entrepreneurial prospects. Entrepreneurship can lead to financial freedom and wealth generation.

Tax Planning:

Consult with a tax specialist to plan your tax approach. Tax-efficient withdrawal strategies in retirement or tax planning for investments are examples of strategies.

Consider how you would like to leave a financial legacy. At this level, estate planning may include trusts, charitable contributions, and generational asset transfer.

Level 4:

Asset Protection

The apex of the wealth-building pyramid is devoted to wealth preservation and protection:

Asset Protection:

Use asset protection measures to secure your wealth from creditors and legal liabilities. Trusts, limited liability corporations (LLCs), and insurance can all be part of your strategy.

Estate Tax Planning:

If you have a considerable amount of wealth, you should talk with an estate planning expert to reduce estate taxes. Gifting, family-limited partnerships, and charity trusts are examples of strategies.

Long-Term Care Planning:

Create a long-term care plan, including insurance or funds for projected future care needs.

Family Wealth Education:
Inform family members about financial responsibility and wealth management. Consider passing on your financial expertise to future generations.

Strategies for Savings and Investing

Now, let's go deeper into tactics for saving and investing, which are critical components of wealth creation.

1.

Increase Retirement Savings
Tax-advantaged retirement funds are among the most effective wealth-building strategies.

Contributions to a 401(k) plan:
If your workplace offers a 401(k) plan, contribute enough to take advantage of any corporate match. This is essentially free money that will help you save for retirement.

Contributions to an Individual Retirement Account (IRA):

If qualified, donate to an IRA. Traditional IRAs provide for tax-deferred accumulation, but Roth IRAs allow for tax-free withdrawals in retirement.

Catch-up Contributions:

If you are over the age of 50, you are eligible for catch-up contributions. For people nearing retirement, both 401(k)s and IRAs allow for increased contributions.

Asset Allocation:

As you get older, review and alter your asset allocation. Younger investors may choose growth equities, but senior investors may prefer a more conservative combination.

2.

Risk Management and Diversification

Diversification is an important risk-management approach for maximizing returns:

Asset Allocation:

Based on your risk tolerance and investment timeframe, choose the appropriate mix of asset types (stocks, bonds, cash, and real estate).

Diversify Within Asset Classes: Diversify more within each asset class. For example, in your stock portfolio, mix large-cap, small-cap, domestic, and international stocks.

Rebalance your portfolio at least once a year to preserve your preferred asset allocation. This guarantees that you are not unduly reliant on a single asset class.

Risk Assessment:

Evaluate your risk tolerance and financial goals on a regular basis. If your circumstances change, you should adjust your portfolio.

3.

Cost-Per-Item Averaging

Dollar-cost averaging (DCA) is an investment technique that includes investing a fixed amount of money at regular periods, regardless of market conditions. DCA can be a helpful tool for reducing market volatility:

Systematic Investing:

Whether the market is up or down, you invest regularly using DCA. This method mitigates the effect of market timing.

DCA can reduce the danger of making a large, ill-timed investment at market peaks.

Automatic Investments:

To make DCA easier to implement, set up automatic contributions to your investment accounts.

4.

Tax-Advantaged Investing

Tax planning is an important aspect of maximizing your investment profits. Consider the following tax-advantaged investment strategies:

Prioritize contributions to tax-advantaged accounts such as 401(k)s, IRAs, and Health Savings Accounts (HSAs).

Tax-loss harvesting is the practice of offsetting capital gains with capital losses by selling investments that have lost value. This may lower your taxable income.

Dividends and Capital Gains:
Invest in assets that qualify for lower dividend and capital gain tax rates. These rates are often lower than those applicable to ordinary income.

Long-Term Investments:
Assets kept for more than a year frequently obtain favorable tax treatment. To profit from lower long-term capital gains rates, consider a buy-and-hold approach.

5
. Risk Control
It is critical to safeguard your savings and financial well-being:

Maintain an emergency fund to cover unforeseen needs and to prevent having to liquidate investments during a downturn.

Insurance: Check and update your insurance co
verage on a regular basis. Adequate health, auto, house, and liability insurance can protect your assets.

Estate Planning:
Create or amend your estate plan to guarantee that your assets and investments are allocated in accordance with your intentions. This can also help to reduce taxes and legal fees.

Advanced Wealth Creation Techniques

As your wealth-building adventure progresses, you may want to look into more complex tactics. Here are a few to think about:

1.

   Investing in Real Estate

Real estate may be a great tool for accumulating wealth. Among the investment alternatives are:

Rental properties can provide a source of passive income as well as possible property appreciation.

REITs (Real Estate Investment Trusts): REITs are publicly traded businesses that hold or finance income-producing real estate in a variety of property industries. They allow you to invest in real estate without owning any physical assets.

Crowdfunding for Real Estate:
   Online platforms allow investors to pool their funds to invest in real estate projects. This can provide you access to real estate opportunities that demand less financing.

2.

   Investment Strategies
   As your financial knowledge expands, you may want to investigate sophisticated stock market methods such as:

Value investing is locating inexpensive stocks and holding them for the long term. Value investors seek stocks with good fundamentals that are trading at a low price.

Dividend Growth Investing:
Look for equities from firms that have a history of increasing dividends consistently. This technique can give a regular source of income in retirement.

Trading Options:
Options can be used to generate money or as a hedging strategy. They do, however, carry a higher level of danger and complexity.

3.
Business ownership
Starting and running a business can be a path to wealth creation if you have a business idea or an entrepreneurial spirit:

Develop a thorough business plan that details your product or service, target market, competition, and financial projections.

Funding:
Look at other funding possibilities, such as bootstrapping, loans, venture capital, or crowd sourcing.

Scaling:
Concentrate on growing your firm in order to increase sales and profitability. Consider employing new employees, increasing product lines, or venturing into new markets.

4.
Tax Reduction

Tax optimization becomes increasingly crucial as one's wealth increases:

Tax-Advantaged Investments:
   Look into advanced tax-advantaged methods like Opportunity Zones, which offer tax breaks for investments in economically challenged areas.

To maximize deductions, use tax-efficient charitable giving structures such as donor-advised funds or charitable trusts.

Generational money Planning:
   Think about ways to transfer money down to future generations while minimizing estate taxes.

5.
   Estate Planning
   Legacy planning entails carefully transferring wealth to heirs or charitable purposes. Among the possible strategies are:

Trusts:
   Create trusts to safeguard and manage assets for beneficiaries. Trusts can provide asset protection and control.

Generational Wealth Transfer:
   Create a strategy for passing wealth down to future generations. This could include gifting tactics or establishing family foundations.

Charitable Giving:
   Philanthropy allows you to leave a legacy. Create a charity

foundation or donate to existing groups that share your ideals.

Building wealth is a journey that needs dedication, patience, and a commitment to lifelong learning. As you ascend the wealth-building pyramid, keep in mind that success is measured not just by the size of your bank account, but also by the choices and opportunities that wealth provides.

Maintain focus on your financial objectives and adjust your strategies as needed to attain them. Seek financial guidance as needed, and keep in mind that wealth creation is not a solitary undertaking; it may have a good impact on your family, community, and the causes you care about.

Financial Independence and Retirement Planning

Financial Independence and Retirement Planning

It's now time to take a break from the daily grind and enjoy the results of our labor. However, retirement is more than just reaching a specific age; it is also about gaining financial independence and ensuring that you have the resources to sustain the lifestyle you want throughout your retirement years. In this chapter, we'll look at the significance of retirement planning and ways for achieving financial independence.

The Value of Retirement Planning
Retirement planning is not a choice; it is a requirement. Here's why it's so important:

People are living longer lives, which means retirement could last 20, 30, or even 40 years. Adequate savings are required to sustain your preferred lifestyle in retirement.

Limitations of Social Security:
While Social Security is a safety net, it is not intended to replace your whole income. Relying primarily on Social Security

in retirement may result in a reduced standard of living.

Medical Expenses:

Medical expenses tend to rise with age. Proper retirement planning includes factoring in healthcare costs, which can be large.

Inflation:

Inflation diminishes the ability of money to buy more goods . To overcome this, your retirement savings must increase in order to stay pace with escalating expenditures.

Financial Independence:

Retirement preparation is about more than simply survival; it is also about financial independence. You should be able to spend your retirement years anyway you wish without financial restraints.

Setting Retirement Objectives

Setting clear and attainable retirement goals is the first step in retirement planning. Here's how to go about it:

Determine Your Retirement Age: Determine the age at which you want to retire. Your retirement age influences the duration and amount of your retirement funds.

Calculate Your Retirement Expenses: Estimate your retirement expenses, which should include housing, healthcare, daily living expenses, travel, and any other lifestyle expenses you expect. Be thorough while remaining realistic.

Consider Inflation:

When forecasting future spending, keep inflation in mind. An yearly inflation rate of roughly 2-3% is a common rule of thumb.

Consider Social Security:

Figure out how much you'll earn from Social Security. The Social Security Administration's website provides an estimate. Remember that the age at which you begin collecting benefits influences the amount you will get.

Identify Additional Income Sources: Think about any additional retirement income sources, such as pensions, rental income, or part-time work during retirement.

Set Savings Goals:

Determine how much you need to save for retirement based on your projected costs and other sources of income. For assistance, use retirement calculators or speak with a financial professional.

Retirement Plans and Savings Methods

To meet your retirement savings objectives, you'll need to use a variety of retirement accounts as well as effective savings tactics, such as:

Employer-Sponsored Retirement Accounts (ESRAs)

Contribute as much as possible to your 401(k) plan if your workplace offers one, especially if your employer matches contributions. 401(k)s provide tax benefits such as tax-deferred growth and potential employer matching.

403(b):

Non-profit organizations and educational institutions provide 403(b) plans, which are similar to 401(k) plans. They also provide tax advantages.

457(b):

457(b) plans, which allow tax-advantaged retirement savings, are frequently available to government employees.

Individual Retirement Account (IRA):

Contributions to a traditional IRA may be tax-deductible, and investments grow tax-deferred until withdrawn.

Roth IRA:

Roth IRAs provide tax-free retirement withdrawals, but contributions are made after-tax monies. Roth IRAs offer the option of tax-free retirement income.

3. HSA (Health Savings Account)

HSAs are useful for addressing healthcare expenses in retirement. Contributions are tax-deductible, and withdrawals are tax-free for eligible medical costs.

4. Plans for Self-Employed Retirement

If you work for yourself, look into retirement plans such as the Simplified Employee Pension (SEP) IRA or the Solo 401(k). These plans provide tax advantages as well as options for retirement savings.

5. Contributions to Make Up for Lost Time

Take advantage of the catch-up contributions allowed in retirement accounts if you are 50 or older. These additional contributions aid in the acceleration of your retirement savings.

Sixth, Dollar-Cost Averaging

Contribute to retirement accounts on a regular basis using dollar-cost averaging. This method mitigates the impact of market volatility and can result in larger long-term benefits.

7. Diversification of Investments

To spread risk, diversify your retirement account. Consider a portfolio that includes a mix of equities, bonds, and other asset types that correspond to your risk tolerance and retirement time frame

8. Review your retirement savings progress on a regular basis

and change your contributions and investments as appropriate. Life circumstances and financial objectives might shift over time.

9. Clear High-Interest Debt

Pay off high-interest debt first, such as credit cards, before or in addition to retirement funds. Debt reduction reduces financial stress and frees up funds for retirement.

10. Postponing Retirement

If feasible, consider postponing retirement. Working an additional few years might considerably increase your retirement savings and Social Security benefits.

Developing a Retirement Income Strategy

Transition from a savings-focused strategy to an income-focused one as you near retirement. Here's how:

1.

Calculate Your Retirement Income

Estimate your retirement income from all sources, including Social Security, pensions, rental income, and retirement accounts.

2.

Plan Your Withdrawal Strategy

Determine your retirement account withdrawal strategy. A frequent guideline is the 4% rule, which states that you can withdraw 4% of your retirement savings in the first year and adjust for inflation in following years. However, your plan should be tailored to your specific financial condition and objectives.

3.

Think about Annuities

Annuities can give guaranteed income in retirement. Consider if immediate or delayed annuities are better suited to your income need and risk tolerance.

4.

Examine Healthcare Costs

Examine your healthcare requirements and prices. Medicare covers some medical bills, but extra coverage or long-term care insurance may be required.

5.

Tax-Saving Withdrawals

Create a tax-advantaged withdrawal strategy. To minimize taxes in retirement, consider strategically withdrawing from taxable, tax-deferred, and tax-free accounts.

6. Estate Planning

If you want to leave a legacy, make an estate plan that specifies how your assets will be divided. Trusts, wills, and charitable giving schemes are examples of this.

7. Make any necessary adjustments.

As circumstances change, continue to review and alter your retirement income plan. Life events, market conditions, and financial objectives can all have an impact on your strategy.

Social Security Enhancement

For most Americans, Social Security is a critical component of their retirement income. To maximize your Social Security payments, you must plan ahead of time:

Understand your Full Retirement Age (FRA), which is the age at which you can collect full Social Security payments. It differs according on your birth year.

Delayed Retirement Credits: Postponing Social Security benefits beyond your FRA may result in higher monthly payouts. You can receive delayed retirement credits for each year you delay, up to the age of 70.

Spousal Benefits:

Married people can plan their Social Security plans to optimize their benefits. Couples may benefit from strategies such as "file and suspend" and "file and limit."

Survivor Benefits:

Learn about survivor benefits, which can provide financial assistance to a surviving spouse.

Considerations for Taxation: Understand the tax consequences of Social Security benefits. Depending on your overall income, a percentage of your benefits may be subject to taxation.

Retirement Financial Independence

Achieving financial independence in retirement is having the resources to live the lifestyle you want without worrying about money. Here are some important considerations:

Retirement Lifestyle:

Define financial independence for yourself. Consider your planned retirement lifestyle, vacation plans, hobbies, and any other things that will offer you delight.

Maintain an emergency reserve even after retirement. Having cash reserves on hand can help you avoid raiding your retirement accounts during market downturns.

Budgeting and Monitoring:

In retirement, you should continue to budget and monitor your costs. Maintaining financial awareness allows you to prevent overspending and ensures that your income lasts.

Healthcare Expenses:

Budget for healthcare expenses such as Medicare premiums, supplemental insurance, and anticipated long-term care bills.

Inflation Adjustments:
Think about how inflation will affect your retirement income over time. Adjust your withdrawal strategy as needed.

Legacy Planning:
If you want to leave a financial legacy, you should make or amend your estate plan to match your preferences.

Stay Active and Engaged:
Retirement isn't only about money; it's also about making the most of your newfound freedom. Maintaining a meaningful lifestyle in retirement requires staying active, engaged, and mentally occupied.

Avoiding Common Retirement Pitfalls

While retirement planning is critical, it is also critical to avoid common errors that might compromise your financial security:

Underestimation of Expenses:
Be honest with yourself about your retirement expenses. Failure to plan for unforeseen costs can result in financial stress.

Overdependence on Social Security: While Social Security is important, it should not be your entire source of income. Diversify your sources of retirement income.

Neglecting Healthcare Costs:
In retirement, healthcare costs tend to climb. Plan for these expenses and think about long-term care insurance.

Ignoring Taxes:
Understand the tax consequences of your retirement income sources and plan tax-efficient withdrawals.

Market Timing:
Do not make major investment adjustments solely on short-term market volatility. Long-term thinking is essential.

Excessive Debt:
Try to reach retirement with as little high-interest debt as possible. Debt repayment in retirement might put a strain on your finances.

Retirement planning is a complex process that entails defining specific goals, actively saving, and devising an income distribution scheme for your retirement years. Financial independence in retirement means being able to live your life without worrying about money.

As you make your way from debt to wealth, keep in mind that retirement planning is an important part of reaching ultimate financial independence. Take the time to evaluate your retirement goals, investigate your options, and seek professional advice as needed. You can look forward to a retirement that is not just financially secure but also rewarding and joyful with careful preparation and diligent saving.

Wealth-Building Tax Strategies

Wealth-Building Tax Strategies

Taxes are unavoidable in our financial lives, but they don't have to be a hardship. You may improve your financial status, lower your tax bill, and accelerate your journey to wealth with proper tax planning and methods. This chapter will look at different tax techniques that can help you keep more of your hard-earned money and develop wealth more efficiently.

The Value of Tax Planning

It entails comprehending the tax implications of your financial actions and taking legal procedures to reduce your tax liability. Effective tax preparation can offer a number of major advantages:

Increased Savings:

By lowering your tax burden, you have more money to save, invest, and expand your wealth.

Compound Growth:

The money saved on taxes can be invested, allowing it to compound over time.

Lower taxes imply more money in your pocket each year, which improves your monthly cash flow.

Financial Security:
Tax preparation can assist you in preserving your wealth and ensuring your financial future.

Legacy Planning:
Tax techniques that are effective can also help with estate planning, allowing you to pass on more of your money to your descendants.

Now, let's look at several essential tax methods that can help you on your way to wealth.

1.

Tax-Advantaged Investing

Investing is a great instrument for growing wealth, and how you invest can have a major impact on your tax liability. Here are some tax-advantaged investment strategies:

a.

Asset Positioning
Asset location is the smart placement of your investments in tax-advantaged and taxable accounts. As an example:

Consider holding tax-inefficient investments, such as bonds

and actively managed funds, in tax-advantaged accounts (such as IRAs and 401(k)s). These accounts provide tax-free growth.

Taxable Accounts:
Place tax-efficient investments in taxable accounts, such as index funds or tax-managed funds. There are fewer taxable events as a result of these investments.

b.
Revenue-Loss Harvesting

Tax-loss harvesting entails selling investments that have decreased in value in order to offset capital gains and lower your tax burden. This method is particularly useful in taxable brokerage accounts.

c.
Capital Gains and Qualified Dividends
Invest in assets that are eligible for lower tax rates on dividends and capital gains. Long-term capital gains and qualified dividends are often taxed at lower rates than ordinary income.

d.
Tax-Exempt Funds
Consider investing in tax-efficient funds. These funds seek to minimize capital gains distributions in order to reduce your tax liability.

f.
Waiting Periods
Long-term investments (kept for more than a year) frequently

obtain preferential tax treatment over short-term investments. Consider this when developing your investment strategy.

2.

Tax Deferral and Retirement Accounts

One of the most efficient methods to decrease your current tax liability and build wealth for the future is to use retirement funds. Here's how:

a.

401(k)s and Individual Retirement Accounts

Contributions to 401(k)s and traditional IRAs are frequently tax-deductible, lowering your taxable income in the year you make the contribution. These accounts also provide tax-deferred growth, which means you don't have to pay taxes on gains until you withdraw the money in retirement.

b.

Roth IRAs and Roth 401(k) accounts

While Roth contributions are made after-tax monies, withdrawals in retirement are tax-free. Roth accounts can give tax-free income throughout retirement, which is especially useful if you expect to be in a higher tax band later in life.

c.

Employer Connections

Utilize employer matching contributions in your workplace retirement plan (e.g., 401(k)). Employer contributions are effectively free money that can considerably increase your retirement savings.

d.

RMDs (Required Minimum Distributions)

RMDs for traditional retirement funds should be considered. You must withdraw a minimum amount each year once you reach a certain age (typically 72).

e.

Penalties for Early Withdrawal

When feasible, avoid early withdrawals from retirement accounts. Withdrawals made before the age of 5912 are usually subject to penalties and taxes.

3.

Tax-Affordable Withdrawal Methods

The manner in which you withdraw funds in retirement may have an influence on your tax liability. Consider the following strategies:

a. Tax Bracket Administration

Manage your withdrawals to stay in a low-tax bracket. This may entail taking distributions from taxable, tax-deferred, and tax-free funds.

b.

Conversion to Roth

Consider Roth conversions if it makes financial sense. This entails converting traditional IRA holdings to Roth IRA assets and paying taxes on the conversion amount. Future Roth IRA withdrawals are tax-free.

c.

Postpone Social Security.

Delaying Social Security benefits may boost your monthly payouts while perhaps reducing the requirement for taxable withdrawals from retirement accounts in your early retirement years.

d.

Use Tax-Exempt Funds.

Continue to employ tax-efficient investments in retirement accounts to reduce taxable events.

e.

Revenue-Loss Harvesting

Even in retirement, you can employ tax-loss harvesting to offset gains and cut taxes.

HSAs (Health Savings Accounts)

HSAs are useful not only for medical bills, but also as a tax-advantaged investment vehicle:

Donations are tax deductible.

The HSA investments grow tax-free.

Withdrawals for eligible medical costs are exempt from taxation.

In retirement, you can utilize HSA funds for medical expenses such as Medicare premiums, long-term care premiums, and other eligible expenses, making HSAs a valuable tax-efficient tool.

5.

Charitable Contributions and Tax Deductions

Charitable giving is not only a way to support causes that are important to you, but it is also a tax-efficient strategy:

a.

Itemized Deductions

Charitable contributions can reduce your taxable income if you itemize deductions on your tax return.

b.

Donor-Advised Funds (DAFs)

To optimize your philanthropic contribution deductions, consider establishing a donor-advised fund. You make a contribution to the fund, get a tax break, and then recommend awards to your favorite charity over time.

c.

QCDs (Qualified Charitable Distributions)

If you are 7012 or older, you can make QCDs straight from your IRA to qualifying charities. These distributions contribute to your required minimum distribution (RMD) but are not taxable income.

6.

Planning for Estate and Gift Taxes

Estate planning is essential for passing money down to future generations while reducing estate taxes. Among the key strategies are:

a. Gifting Techniques

Consider making assets available to heirs throughout your lifetime. There are both yearly and lifetime gift tax exclusions to consider. For more information, speak with an estate planning attorney.

b.

Trusteeships

Use trusts to manage and distribute assets as you see fit while reducing estate taxes.

c.

Exclusionary Gifts on an Annual Basis

Use the annual gift tax exclusion to make tax-free gifts to heirs. This exclusion was $15,000 per recipient as of the most recent update in 2021.

d.

Convenience

Spouses can exploit portability laws to effectively combine their inheritance tax exemptions, possibly protecting a larger amount of their wealth from estate taxes.

Structures of Business and Investment

If you own a business or invest in real estate, how you arrange your activities can have serious tax consequences:

a.

Commercial Entities

Based on your individual business goals and tax concerns, choose the right business form, such as an LLC, S corporation, or C corporation.

b.

Property Investment

Investigate tax-advantaged real estate investing strategies such as 1031 exchanges, which allow you to postpone capital gains taxes while selling one investment property and purchasing another.

c.

Impairment
Utilize depreciation deductions for real estate assets to minimize taxable income.

d.

Active vs. Passive Income
Understand the difference between passive and active income since tax treatment differs. Consider how you might structure your investments to maximize tax efficiency.

Tax breaks and incentives
Examine the following tax credits and incentives to see if they apply to your situation:

a.

Credits for Education

Consider the American Opportunity Tax Credit (AOTC) or the Lifetime Learning Credit to offset college expenses if you have children in college.

b.

Credits for Energy Efficiency

Energy-efficient house renovations, such as solar panels or energy-efficient windows, are eligible for tax credits.

c.

Child Tax Credit

Families with dependent children may be eligible for the Child Tax Credit, which lowers your tax liability.

d.

Credits for Research and Development (R&D)

Businesses that conduct R&D may be eligible for tax breaks that reward innovation.

e.

Tax Credits for Small Businesses

Investigate tax breaks for small firms, such as the Small Business Health Care Tax Credit.

9.

Professional Advice

Tax regulations are complicated and subject to rapid change. Consider hiring a tax professional or financial advisor who can give specialized tax planning and keep you up to date on tax legislation changes.

Avoiding Common Tax Pitfalls

While tax planning is critical, it is also critical to avoid major tax pitfalls:

Procrastination:
   Don't put off your tax planning until the last minute. Effective tax planning needs time and thought.

Ignoring Deductions:
   Be sure to claim all eligible deductions and credits. Overpaying taxes might occur from overlooking deductions.

Failure to Adjust:
   As your life circumstances evolve, so should your tax plan. Review and alter your plan as needed on a regular basis.

Ignoring State Taxes: Keep in mind that state tax laws differ. Consider state income taxes as well as any special tax breaks or credits available in your state.

Ignoring Retirement Accounts: Contribute as much as possible to retirement accounts to take advantage of tax-deferred growth and potential tax deductions.

Ignoring specialist Advice:
   Complex tax issues may necessitate the assistance of a tax specialist. Always seek for advice.

Tax planning is an essential component of your financial transformation from debt to prosperity. You may optimize your financial status, decrease your tax bill, and expedite your wealth-building efforts by knowing and executing efficient tax methods. Keep in mind that tax regulations are subject to change, so keep informed and adjust your tax plan as needed. You may keep more of your money and develop wealth more effectively with a proactive approach to tax preparation, taking you one step closer to financial independence and security.

The Importance of Continuous Learning and Growth

The Importance of Continuous Learning and Growth

As you engage on the journey of financial transformation, one of the most powerful assets you can build is your own knowledge and personal development. In this chapter, we'll look at the transforming potential of ongoing learning and growth. We'll look at how a commitment to broadening your experiences, refining your talents, and nurturing your personal growth may not only boost your financial success but also enrich every aspect of your life.

The Changing Knowledge Landscape

Knowledge in the modern world is not static; it is a dynamic and ever-changing thing. Staying informed, adaptive, and intellectually interested is critical for negotiating the challenges of modern life. This is especially true in the financial sector, where markets, laws, and economic conditions are constantly changing.

The Advantages of Lifelong Learning and Growth

Continuous learning and development provide numerous

benefits that extend far beyond the field of finance. Here are a few important advantages:

Financial Empowerment:
  Lifelong learning provides you with the information and skills to make sound financial decisions. It enables you to effectively understand difficult financial concepts, manage your finances, and prepare for the future.

Adaptability:
  In a quickly changing environment, adaptability is a valuable quality. Continuous learning guarantees that you can pivot, adopt new technology, and prosper in changing circumstances.

job progression:
  Learning and excelling in your field can lead to job progression and higher income possibilities. It establishes you as a valued asset to companies and clients.

Personal fulfillment comes from learning new things and achieving personal goals. They add to a sense of purpose and well-being.

Problem-Solving:
  Lifelong learners are superior problem solvers. They can assess situations, think critically, and devise creative solutions to problems.

Expanded Horizons:
  Learning exposes you to new ideas, cultures, and viewpoints. It broadens your perspectives and improves your capacity to

connect with people from other backgrounds.

The Road to Lifelong Learning and Growth

Now that we understand the significance of ongoing learning and development, let us look at how to engage on this transforming journey:

1. Establish Specific Goals

Begin by establishing explicit learning objectives. What are your goals? Whether it's learning a new skill, gaining a certification, or simply reading more books, having defined objectives provides your learning meaning and direction.

2. Embrace Curiosity

Develop a curious mindset. Ask questions, seek answers, and investigate issues that actually interest you. Curiosity is the fuel that propels lifelong learning.

3. Diversify Your Learning Resources

Don't rely on just one source of information. Look into books, online courses, podcasts, seminars, and mentorship. Each source brings a distinct perspective and body of knowledge.

4. Develop a Learning Routine

Create a regular learning habit. Making consistent improvement requires consistency.

5. Read widely

Reading is one of the most accessible and effective ways to learn. Read books, articles, and periodicals on a variety of themes, such as finance, personal development, science, and the arts.

6. Use Technology

Make use of technology to enhance learning. Online classes, webinars, and educational applications are all convenient ways to learn new skills and knowledge.

7. Seek Feedback and Mentorship

Don't be reluctant to seek comments from peers, mentors, or professionals in your area. Constructive feedback assists you in identifying areas for improvement and refining your talents.

8. Join Learning Communities

Participate in both online and offline learning groups. Participate in forums, discussion groups, or workshops where you may share your knowledge and learn from others.

9. Pursue Formal Education

Consider formal education if it aligns with your goals. Whether it's seeking a degree or obtaining professional certifications, formal education can open opportunities and expand your knowledge.

10.

Document Your Learning Journey

Keep a journal or digital record of your learning journey. Keep track of your discoveries, insights, and development. This is a great resource and incentive.

11.

Accept Failure

Don't be afraid of failure; accept it as a necessary part of the learning process. Mistakes and failures bring vital lessons and opportunity for growth.

12.

Push Yourself

In the face of adversity, learning thrives. Take on initiatives or tasks that need you to learn new skills or expertise.

13.

Maintain your curiosity

Maintain a spirit of wonder and inquisitiveness about the universe. Approach each day with an open mind and a desire to learn something new.

14.

Teach Others

Teaching is a great approach to consolidate your own expertise. Share what you've learnt with others by mentoring, writing, or public speaking.

15.

Reflect and Iterate

Consider your learning journey on a regular basis. What have you accomplished? What do you want to learn next? Use this self-evaluation to fine-tune your learning objectives.

The Importance of Learning in Financial Success

Continuous learning is very important in finance.

Ways education add to financial success:

Financial Literacy:
Learning about personal finance, budgeting, investing, and financial planning equips you to make sound financial decisions. It assists you in avoiding typical financial traps and optimizing your financial tactics.

Investment Knowledge:
A thorough understanding of investment principles enables you to construct and manage a diverse investment portfolio. You can make decisions that are consistent with your financial objectives and risk tolerance.

Risk Management:
Understanding risk management tactics in finance will help you preserve your assets and navigate economic challenges.

Income Growth:
Continuous learning and skill improvement can lead to job growth and increased earning potential.

Entrepreneurship:
As an entrepreneur, you must always learn to stay competitive, innovate, and develop your business.

Financial Planning:

Learning about financial planning allows you to define clear financial goals, create a route to attain them, and alter your plan as circumstances change.

Tax Optimization:
Understanding tax laws and tactics can help you reduce your tax liability and keep more of your money.

Economic Awareness:
Staying updated about economic trends and worldwide events allows you to make strategic financial decisions in response to changing market conditions.

Challenges and Overcoming Them
While the benefits of lifelong learning and growth are enormous, it is critical to recognize and solve frequent challenges:

Time Constraints:
Many people mention a lack of time as a barrier to learning. To overcome this, prioritize learning in your daily schedule and explore effective learning methods.

Information Overload:
In the digital era, information overload can be daunting. Concentrate on quality above quantity, and curate your learning resources.

Procrastination is a typical barrier to learning. To combat it, divide your learning objectives into smaller, achievable tasks and set deadlines.

Motivation:

Maintaining motivation can be difficult. To stay motivated, link your learning objectives to your larger life goals.

Fear of Failure: Fear of failure can stop you from taking risks and accepting new challenges. Remember that failure is a natural part of the learning process and a chance for improvement.

A Lifelong Growth Journey

Never underestimate the transforming power of ongoing learning and growth in the pursuit of financial success and a satisfying life. It's a never-ending quest with benefits that go far beyond money. By cultivating your intellectual curiosity, learning new skills, and keeping open to the world's ever-changing information, you not only improve your financial chances but also enrich your life in incalculable ways. In the words of the great philosopher Socrates, "education is the kindling of a flame, not the filling of a vessel." May your flame of inquiry and progress burn brightly on your lifelong learning journey, illuminating your path to financial prosperity and personal joy.

Protecting Your Wealth

Insurance and Risk Management

Building wealth is a wonderful objective, but it's also vital to preserve your financial well-being along the way. Life is full of unexpected events, and without the necessary precautions in place, your hard-earned money may be vulnerable to a range of hazards. In this chapter, we will look at the main aspects of insurance and risk management, providing you with the knowledge and methods you need to secure your financial future.

The Importance of Insurance and Risk Management

Before delving into the technicalities of insurance and risk management, it's vital to understand why these components are critical to your financial plan:

Financial Loss Protection:
Insurance functions as a safety net, supporting you in lessening the financial impact of unexpected events such as accidents, illness, natural disasters, or the death of a loved one.

Wealth Preservation: Insurance can protect your savings and

investments from depletion in the event of major expenses or liabilities.

Peace of Mind:

Knowing that you are financially safe against unforeseen threats can bring you peace of mind, allowing you to focus on your wealth-building goals with confidence.

Estate Planning:

Insurance can help with estate planning by ensuring that your assets are handed to heirs quickly and with minimal tax consequences.

Let's take a look at the basic components of insurance and risk management to help you make informed decisions and efficiently protect your cash.

1. Health Insurance

Health insurance is a vital aspect of financial well-being since it protects you and your family from the high costs of medical care.

a. Coverage Options

Employer-Sponsored Plans: Many employers incorporate health insurance as part of their benefits package. These plans usually provide an acceptable blend of coverage and cost, with the employer contributing a portion of the premium.

Individual or Family Plans:

If your job does not provide health insurance or you are self-employed, you can purchase individual or family plans through the Health Insurance Marketplace or private insurers.

Government Programs:
   Based on your financial situation, you may be entitled for government programs such as Medicare.

b. Coverage Options
   HMO (Health Maintenance Organization): HMO plans require you to choose a primary care physician and frequently offer reduced costs, but you will need to see specialists through referrals.

PPO (Preferred Provider Organization) plans provide greater flexibility in selecting healthcare providers and specialists, but may have higher premiums and out-of-pocket costs.

HDHP (High-Deductible Health Plan): HDHPs feature lower premiums and are typically paired with Health Savings Accounts (HSAs) for tax benefits.

Catastrophic insurance is designed for young, healthy people and covers major medical events.

c. Deductibles and out-of-pocket expenses
   Understand your plan's deductible, copayments, and coinsurance. The deductible is the amount you pay out of pocket before insurance coverage kicks in.

d. Network Coverage
   Check to determine if your preferred healthcare providers are

in-network, as using out-of-network physicians can result in higher rates.

f. Health Savings Accounts (HSAs)

Consider contributing to an HSA if you have an HDHP. HSAs offer tax advantages and can be used to pay for qualifying medical expenses.

2.

Life Insurance

Life insurance provides financial security to your loved ones in the event of your death. It's an essential component, especially if you have dependents. The following are the primary types of life insurance:

a. Term Life Insurance

It has a death benefit but no monetary value.

Premiums for term life insurance are frequently lower than for other types of life insurance.

b. Whole Life Insurance

Whole life insurance covers you for the rest of your life.

It features a savings component (cash value) that grows over time and can be borrowed from or withdrawn from.

Premiums are higher than for term life insurance.

c. Universal Life Insurance

Flexible premium payment and death benefit options are available with universal life insurance.

There is also a cash value component that may be invested in.

Premiums may fluctuate and climb over time.

d. Considerations

Your financial ambitions and the demands of your beneficiaries influence the type of life insurance you choose.

Determine your coverage needs based on parameters such as your income, debts, and future financial obligations (e.g., mortgage, college expenses).

Examine your life insurance policy on a frequent basis to confirm that it is still applicable to your current position.

3. Disability Insurance

Disability insurance protects your income if you are unable to work due to illness or injury. It's a key safeguard to ensure you can continue to meet your financial obligations. Here's everything you need to know:

a. Short-Term vs. Long-Term Disability Insurance

Short-term provides coverage for a fixed length of time, typically a few months to a year while Long-term coverage for a long period of time

b. Employer Coverage

Some companies incorporate disability insurance as part of their benefits package.

Examine the terms and coverage limitations of your employer-provided disability insurance to ensure it meets your needs.

c. Individual Disability Insurance

If your employer does not provide disability insurance or you desire greater coverage, consider purchasing an individual disability insurance policy.

d. Benefit Amount and Waiting Period

Calculate the amount of benefit required to replace a portion of your income in the event of incapacity.

Consider the waiting period (elimination period) before benefits begin, as it can affect premium prices.

f. Own-Occupation vs. Any-Occupation

Look for disability insurance with a "own-occupation" definition of disability, which means you're pronounced disabled if you can't do the duties of your specific job.

4. Property and Casualty Insurance

Property and casualty insurance, sometimes known as house and auto insurance, protects your assets and offers liability coverage. Consider the following:

a. Home Insurance

Home insurance protects your home and personal belongings from damage caused by occurrences such as fire, theft, or natural disasters.

It also includes liability insurance in case someone is injured on your premises.

b. Auto Insurance

Auto insurance provides coverage for vehicle damage as well as liability coverage in the event of an accident.

Legacy and Philanthropy

Making a Long-Term Impact

It is vital to examine not only what you can accumulate throughout your lifetime, but also what you can leave as a lasting legacy as you seek financial freedom and happiness. Legacy and charity are powerful representations of your values and principles, allowing you to make a far-reaching impact. In this chapter, we'll look at the enormous importance of legacy and generosity, and we'll give you ideas and ways for leaving a legacy that will last for generations.

The Importance of Legacies

Beyond tangible assets, legacy includes the values, ethics, and impact you leave for future generations. A well-crafted legacy represents your life's purpose as well as the positive impact you wish to see in the world. This is what it means to leave a legacy:

Values and Beliefs:

Your legacy embodies your core values and beliefs, serving as a testament to what you hold dear in life.

Legacy refers to the influence you have on others through your actions, advice, or donations.

Generational Wealth:

As part of your legacy, you may choose to leave your descendants both financial and intellectual wealth, allowing them to continue on your legacy.

Philanthropy:

Many legacies are linked to charitable endeavors aimed at bettering society or addressing major global issues.

Memories and Narratives:

The memories, narratives, and teachings you pass down to future generations are also part of your legacy.

Legacy Planning Is Critical

The thoughtful and deliberate process of articulating and developing the legacy you want to leave behind is known as legacy planning. It ensures the achievement of your vision's values, resources, and goals. It is impossible to overestimate the importance of legacy planning:

Clarity of Vision:

Legacy planning requires you to clarify your vision and articulate what you hope to achieve with your wealth and influence.

money Preservation:

It ensures that your money is protected and preserved for future generations and philanthropic purposes.

Mitigation of Family Conflicts:

Legacy planning can help to potential heir conflicts by providing specific instructions and setting expectations.

Tax Efficiency:

Strategic legacy planning can cut inheritance taxes while increasing the value of assets left to heirs and charitable organizations.

Sustaining Your Impact: Legacy planning ensures that your charitable efforts will continue to help the causes that are important to you.

Your legacy can inspire others, resulting in a cascade of good change and social impact.

Let us now look at the principles of legacy planning and philanthropy:

1.

State Your Legacy Vision

Defining your vision is the first step in legacy planning. Consider the following self-reflection questions:

What are the most important values and beliefs I want future generations to inherit?

What kind of transformative change do I want to see in my community or on a larger scale?

How can I use my resources, skills, and interests to effect long-term change?

What do I honestly want to be remembered for when all is said and done?

These concepts will form the basis of your legacy strategy.

2.

Estate Planning

Estate planning is an important part of legacy planning since it guarantees that your assets are distributed according to your intentions. Important estate planning considerations include:

Making or changing your will, which describes how your assets will be divided to heirs and charitable organizations.

The ability to create trusts to provide for specific needs of your beneficiaries, such as education or healthcare.

Beneficiaries must be named for retirement accounts, life insurance policies, and other assets.

Beneficiary designations are regularly reviewed and altered to reflect changes in your life's journey.

Collaboration with an estate planning professional to maximize estate tax avoidance and ensure that your legacy plan is in line with your desired legacy.

3.

Wealth Passing Down Through Generations

Consider the following measures if you intend to leave wealth to future generations:

The development of financial responsibility and wise wealth stewardship among your heirs.

Creating trusts or establishing structured gifting plans to meet your descendants' individual needs while protecting assets from mismanagement.

Family meetings or written directions are used to pass along financial goals and practices.

Encouragement and assistance for new business ventures, as well as financial independence for your heirs.

4.

Philanthropy and charitable giving

Philanthropy is a potent tool for exerting long-term and positive influence. To incorporate generosity into your legacy planning, do the following steps:

a. Choosing a Philanthropic Interest

It is vital to identify the causes and organizations that stimulate your interest. Your philanthropic actions should be consistent with your core values and interests.

b. Developing a Donation Strategy

Developing a strategic giving strategy that describes your philanthropic goals, such as the issues you wish to address, the size of your contributions, and the payment schedule.

c) Establish a Charitable Foundation or Fund

To streamline your charitable initiatives and involve your family in the decision-making process, consider establishing a charitable foundation or a donor-advised fund (DAF).

b. Looking for Meaningful Giving

Concentrating on significant and transformative giving rather than spreading resources too broadly increases the effectiveness of your philanthropic efforts.

e. Participate Your Family

Participating in charitable activities as a family creates a sense of community, social responsibility, and solidarity. Inviting young people to engage in decision-making improves their resolve to affect positive change.

f. Considering Legacy Gifts

Investigating long-term legacies such as endowments, scholarships, or grants that support certain programs or projects.

g. Seeking Professional Help

Working with financial advisors and philanthropic specialists ensures that your charity contributions are tax-effective and consistent with your legacy vision.

5.

Charitable foundations and trusts

Charitable trusts and foundations are effective tools for anyone who want to leave a lasting legacy of philanthropy:

a. Remainder Charitable Trust

A RCT enables you to make a gift to the trust while receiving an income stream for the remainder of your life or for a defined amount of time. The residual assets are subsequently given to charitable organizations.

c. Charitable Lead Trust (CLT)

A CLT directs income to a charitable organization for a defined period of time, after which the remaining assets are dispersed to your heirs.

b. Personal Family Trust

By establishing a private family foundation, you can have an immediate and long-term impact on charitable efforts. This involves investment management and grant distribution.

Donor-Advised Fund (DAF)

A DAF is a simpler method to give. You contribute assets to the fund, gain an instant tax benefit, and then push for long-term contributions to your favorite charities.

6.

Socially Responsible Investing

Social impact investing is the practice of dedicating a portion of your investment portfolio to firms and businesses that emphasize social and environmental goals over financial returns. This strategy enables you to align your assets with your charitable goals while potentially generating a financial return.

7.

Wills and Legacy Letters that are Ethical

Legacy letters and ethical wills are sincere ways of communicating your views, life lessons, and wishes to heirs and future generations. These documents offer personal insights and advice that extend beyond the basic transfer of property.

8.

Mentoring and volunteering

Your legacy includes more than just financial donations; it also includes the positive influence you have on others. Volunteering and mentoring enable you to share your knowledge, skills, and experiences with the next generation.

9.

Continuous Evaluation of Your Legacy Plan

Your legacy plan should be flexible enough to accommodate changes in your life, finances, and charity interests. Regularly reviewing and refining your plan ensures that it remains in tune with your shifting vision.

10.

Seek Professional Help

Philanthropy and legacy planning can be difficult to navigate. It is beneficial to consult with financial consultants, estate planning attorneys, and philanthropy professionals when building a thorough and effective legacy strategy.

Avoiding Common Legacy Planning Pitfalls

While legacy planning is a worthwhile endeavor, it is vital to avoid the following frequent pitfalls:

Procrastination:

Postponing legacy planning may result in missed opportunities to shape your legacy.

Insufficient Clarity:

Failure to explain your legacy vision may result in disorganized efforts and ineffective donations.

Disregard for Family Dynamics:

When involving heirs in philanthropic decisions, it is important to acknowledge the intricacies of family relationships and potential conflicts.

Failure to Seek Professional Counsel: The complexity of charity and legacy planning frequently necessitate the assistance of financial and legal specialists.

Overlooking Tax Implications: Understanding the tax implications of charitable giving and generational asset transfer is crucial.

Philanthropy and legacy are the pinnacle of a well-lived life. By planning your legacy and donating resources to society, you can leave an everlasting imprint that will remain far beyond your lifetime. Legacy planning and philanthropy encompass more than simply financial resources; they also contain the views, ideas, and positive change that you pass down to future generations. Consider how you may help the world and inspire future generations as you work your way from debt to wealth, leaving a legacy of compassion, generosity, and social conscientiousness. Your legacy illustrates wealth's enduring potential to effect positive change in the world.

Financial Resilience in Life Transitions

Financial Resilience in Life Transitions

Life is a journey punctuated by transitions—significant shifts that can affect our circumstances, priorities, and financial environment. In this chapter, we will look at the art of navigating life transitions with financial resilience. Whether it's marriage, parenting, career changes, retirement, or unanticipated problems, the capacity to adapt and make smart financial decisions during these transitions is critical. We will look at ways to not just survive but also prosper in the face of these changes.

Understanding Life Transitions

Life transitions are watershed occasions that usher in transformation. They can be planned or unplanned, pleasant or difficult, and they frequently have financial consequences. Some common life transitions are:

Marriage:
The combination of two lives can have substantial financial effects, such as collaborative financial planning, asset consolidation, and shared financial aspirations.

Parenthood is a life-changing event that includes financial

issues such as daycare expenditures, education preparation, and reevaluating insurance and estate arrangements.

Career Changes:

Changing jobs, establishing a new career, or starting a business can have an influence on income, benefits, and retirement planning.

Retirement:

The journey to retirement include managing savings, assets, and lifestyle modifications to provide financial security in your post-work years.

Divorce:

The breakdown of a marriage can result in complex financial concerns such as asset distribution, alimony, child support, and changed financial goals.

Loss of a Loved One:

Coping with the loss of a spouse or family member can provide financial issues linked to estate settlement, inheritance, and financial independence.

Health concerns:

Managing health concerns can put a strain on finances due to medical bills, insurance claims, and prospective changes in earning capacity.

Education:

Pursuing further education or supporting a child's education necessitates financial planning for tuition, living expenses, and student loans.

Housing Changes:
Buying a home, relocating, or downsizing have an impact on housing costs, mortgages, and property investments.

The Importance of Financial Resilience
The ability to adapt to life's changes, absorb shocks, and preserve financial stability is known as financial resilience. Here's why:

Financial resilience promotes peace of mind during transitions, lowering anxiety and stress.

Flexibility:
It helps you to modify your financial plans to changing circumstances, such as changing employment or starting a family.

Security:
Financial resilience protects against unexpected expenses, ensuring you have a safety net in case of an emergency.

Long-Term Goals:
It keeps long-term financial goals on track, such as retirement planning and wealth creation.

Quality of Life:

Being financially resilient means that you can keep your desired lifestyle even during difficult times.

Protection:

It protects your family's financial well-being, especially during unexpected circumstances like illness or disability.

Financial Resilience Strategies for Life Transitions

Now, let's look at some techniques for developing and strengthening financial resilience during life transitions:

1. Comprehensive Financial Planning

The basis of financial resiliency is a sound financial plan. Begin with:

Setting Specific Goals:

Determine your short- and long-term financial objectives, such as retirement, property, education, and so on.

Budgeting:

Make a precise budget to manage your income, expenses, and savings. This allows you to more effectively allocate resources.

Build an emergency fund to cover at least three to six months of living expenses. It serves as a safety net in the event of an unforeseen event.

Debt Management:

Create a plan to manage and reduce any existing debts, such

as credit card balances or student loans.

Insurance:
Review your insurance coverage, including health, life, disability, and property insurance. Make sure it meets your present and anticipated demands.

Estate Planning:
Create or revise your estate plan, which includes wills, trusts, and powers of attorney, to preserve your assets and provide for your loved ones.

investing Strategy:
Create an investing strategy that is in line with your financial objectives, risk tolerance, and time horizon.

2. Adaptability and Flexibility
Life rarely follows a straight line, and transitions can be unpredictable. Develop adaptability by doing the following:

Scenario Planning:
Consider different life scenarios and their financial implications. Having backup plans can help with the adjustment.

Regular Reviews:
Assess your financial strategy on a regular basis and make improvements as appropriate.

Lifelong Learning:

Stay current on financial techniques, market movements, and tax legislation. Knowledge is a significant tool for flexibility.

3. Communication

Effective communication is critical, especially when life transitions involve others, such as a spouse or family members. Here's how you approach it:

Maintain open and honest conversation with your spouse or partner about financial goals, expectations, and tactics.

Involve family members in financial discussions, especially when it comes to estate planning and caregiving responsibilities.

Financial advisors, attorneys, and other professionals can provide assistance and clarity during difficult transitions.

4. Risk Management

Risk management is critical to financial resiliency. Take the following precautions to protect yourself:

Insurance:
Make sure you have adequate coverage for health, disability, life, and property. Policies should be reviewed on a regular basis to ensure that they are up to current.

Continue to develop and manage an emergency fund to handle unforeseen expenses.

Estate Planning:

Address potential hazards through estate planning, which includes wills, trusts, and advanced directives for healthcare decisions.

Legal Agreements:
Consider legal agreements such as prenuptial or cohabitation agreements to protect assets in the event of divorce or separation.

5. Ongoing Learning and Skill Development
Continuous learning improves your ability to navigate life adjustments. Accept the following strategies:

Enhancement of Skills:
Identify and develop skills that are relevant to your career and financial goals. This can boost income potential and job stability.

Financial literacy entails staying informed about financial matters such as investing techniques, taxes, and retirement planning.

schooling Planning:
Put money aside for your own or your child's schooling. Investigate tax-advantaged savings accounts such as 529 programs.

6. Diversify Your Income Sources
It is dangerous to rely exclusively on one source of income. Diversify your revenue by:

Multiple Income Streams:

Look into opportunities for other income streams such as freelance employment, rental properties, or investments.

Investment Income:

Build a diversified investment portfolio that creates income, such as dividends or rental income.

7. Support Networks

During transitions, rely on your support network. These networks may include:

Family and friends:

Seek emotional and practical support from loved ones at difficult times.

Professional Advisors:

Develop relationships with financial advisors, attorneys, and accountants who can provide professional advice.

Explore community resources and organizations that provide aid during life transitions, such as support groups or counseling services.

8. Self-care and well-being

Maintaining physical and emotional well-being is critical for financial resiliency. Prioritize self-care by:

A healthy lifestyle consists of eating well, exercising regularly, and getting adequate sleep. A healthy body and mind are better suited to deal with stress and obstacles.

Mental Health:

Seek expert help if you are suffering from mental health difficulties. Addressing these issues can help you avoid having a negative influence on your finances.

Time Management: Manage your time properly to reduce stress and maintain a work-life balance.

9. Retirement Planning

While retirement may appear distant during many life transitions, it is critical to plan for it. Here's how to do it:

Contribute to retirement funds such as 401(k)s and IRAs even during moments of transition.

Retirement Budget:

Estimate your retirement expenses and design a budget that represents your expected lifestyle.

Healthcare Planning:

Consider healthcare costs in retirement and look into solutions such as health savings accounts (HSAs) or Medicare.

10. Seek Professional Advice

Seek expert help when making challenging financial decisions during life transitions:

Financial Advisor:

Speak with a financial advisor to assist you manage investment strategies, retirement planning, and general financial well-being.

Estate Attorney:
Consult with an estate planning attorney to verify that your estate plan is up to date and in accordance with your intentions.

Consider hiring a career counselor or coach to assist you navigate the employment market and make educated decisions.

Common Obstacles and How to Overcome Them

Life transitions can be difficult, and financial resilience may be tested. Here are some common difficulties and solutions:

Emotional Stress:
Transitions can cause emotional stress. Seek help from friends, family, or a therapist to manage your emotions properly.

Financial Instability:
Sudden upheavals, such as job loss or divorce, can lead to financial insecurity. Rely on your emergency fund and make a financial plan to get back on track.

Uncertainty:
Transitions in life are frequently fraught with uncertainty. Concentrate on what you can manage, such as your financial decisions and adaptability.

Legal Difficulties:

Legal parts of transitions, such as divorce or estate preparation, can be complicated. Consult with attorneys who specialize in these areas.

Maintain strong social relationships and seek guidance from credible sources to help you make educated decisions.

Embracing Change with Confidence

Life transitions are unavoidable, and their financial consequences can be significant. However, with careful planning, adaptability, and a dedication to financial resilience, you may handle these shifts with confidence. Each shift is an opportunity for growth and a chance to connect your financial decisions with your changing life goals. By embracing change and managing your finances proactively, you may thrive in the face of life's transitions and continue on your path to financial success and fulfillment. Remember that life's twists and turns are all part of the adventure, and with resilience, you may emerge stronger and more prepared for whatever comes your way.

Financial Independence and Beyond

Leaving a Legacy

We've covered everything from budgeting and saving to investing and retirement planning in previous chapters. As we near the end of this journey toward financial wisdom, it is critical that we examine a pinnacle achievement in the world of finance: financial independence and the development of a lasting legacy.

The Road to Financial Independence

Financial freedom is a significant milestone in your financial journey. It denotes the point at which you have amassed enough money and passive income streams to support your desired lifestyle without relying on employment or active revenue. Achieving financial independence allows you to make decisions based on your passions, values, and personal objectives rather than financial need.

The Importance of Financial Independence

Financial freedom is about more than just earning riches; it is about gaining control over your life. Here's why:

Financial independence allows you to pursue your passions,

travel, spend time with loved ones, or engage in things that bring you joy without being bound by a 9-to-5 schedule.

Security:

It acts as a safety net against unforeseen financial setbacks such as medical costs or economic downturns.

Reduced Stress:

Financial independence decreases financial stress and anxiety, allowing you to focus on your physical and emotional well-being.

Generational Wealth:

Financial independence allows you to leave a lasting legacy for future generations, making a beneficial impact that lasts beyond your lifetime.

Philanthropy:

It enables you to engage in philanthropic initiatives and support causes close to your heart.

Financial Independence Strategies

Financial independence is feasible with the appropriate tactics and dedication. Here are some important actions to assist you attain this goal:

1. Establish Specific Goals

Define your financial independence objectives. Consider

aspects such as the age at which you want to attain it, your desired lifestyle, and any specific financial goals.

2. Create a Comprehensive Financial Plan

Create a precise financial strategy that includes:
   Goals for Savings and Investing: Determine how much you need to save and invest to achieve financial freedom.

Budgeting:
   Make a realistic budget that allows you to save and invest a large amount of your income.

Debt Management:
   Address any outstanding bills and work toward becoming debt-free.

Build an emergency fund to handle unforeseen needs without jeopardizing your financial progress.

3. Increase your earnings
   Increasing your income can hasten your path to financial freedom. Consider the following approaches:

Career Advancement:
   Look for prospects for advancement, promotions, or higher-paying jobs.

Side Hustles:
   Look into side companies or freelance employment to boost your income.

Investment Income:

Create a diverse investment portfolio that creates passive income in the form of dividends, interest, or rental income.

4. Invest Wisely

Investing is a crucial driver of financial freedom. Create a solid investment strategy that is in line with your goals, risk tolerance, and time horizon. Diversify your investments to spread risk and increase profits.

5. Save and live within your means

Saving a significant amount of your salary is a core element of reaching financial independence. Live within your means, prioritize saving, and minimize superfluous purchases.

6. Improve Tax Efficiency

Investigate tax-advantaged accounts and ways to reduce your tax liability, such as retirement accounts (e.g., 401(k) and IRA) and tax-efficient investments.

7. Ongoing Education

Keep up with personal finance, investing methods, and economic developments. Knowledge is a key tool for making sound financial decisions.

8th. Periodic Evaluation

Examine your financial plan and progress toward financial freedom on a regular basis. Adjust your strategies as needed to stay on track.

9. Consider Healthcare Costs

Include healthcare costs in your financial strategy, especially as you near retirement. To reduce these costs, look into health savings accounts (HSAs) and long-term care insurance.

10. Create Multiple Income Streams

Diversify your revenue sources to lessen your dependency on a single source. This can be rental income, dividend stocks, royalties, or online enterprises.

11. Estate Planning

As you approach financial independence, comprehensive estate planning becomes increasingly important. Consider the following:

Wills and Trusts:

Make or alter your will and establish trusts to ensure that your assets are dispersed according to your intentions.

Power of Attorney:

Appoint someone you trust to make financial and medical decisions on your behalf if you become incapacitated.

Beneficiary Designations:

Review and amend beneficiary designations on accounts and insurance policies.

12. Consider Philanthropy.

Consider how you may incorporate generosity into your financial independence quest. Charitable giving can be a satisfying part of your legacy.

13. Seek Professional Advice

Consult with financial advisors and estate planning professionals to ensure your financial strategy matches with your
goals and protects your assets for future generations.

14. The Influence of Legacy

Financial freedom, while crucial, is only one component of your
financial path. Beyond this, there is the possibility to leave a
lasting legacy—a positive and lasting impact on the world and
the people you care about.

15. Different Kinds of Legacies

Your legacy consists of more than simply financial assets. It
includes the beliefs, principles, and good effect you leave behind.
Here are some examples of legacy:

Financial Legacy:

This comprises the wealth and assets you leave to heirs,
charitable organizations, or causes you support.

Intellectual Legacy:

Your intellectual legacy includes the knowledge, skills, and
wisdom you share with others through mentoring, teaching, or
writing.

Philanthropic Legacy:

Many people seek to leave a philanthropic legacy by supporting charity causes, founding foundations, or endowing
scholarships.

Family heritage:
Your family heritage includes the values, traditions, and tales you pass down to future generations. It shapes your family's personality and identity.

Leaving a Legacy
Leaving a lasting legacy needs careful planning and forethought. Here's how you can leave a lasting legacy:

1. Determine Your Values and Priorities
Begin by defining the values and principles that are most important to you. What causes or topics are close to your heart? What kind of constructive impact do you wish to have on the world?

2. Establish Specific Philanthropic Goals
Establish specific charitable goals if philanthropy is part of your legacy. Determine the causes or organizations you want to support and plan your donating strategy.

3. Involve Your Family
Engage your family in discussions regarding your legacy. Share your principles and philanthropic aims with them, and encourage their participation and input.

4. Make a Legacy Plan
Create a thorough legacy strategy that includes the following elements:

Estate Planning:
Make sure your will, trusts, and beneficiary designations are

in line with your legacy plans.

Set up structures for philanthropic giving, such as a family foundation, donor-advised fund, or charitable trust.

Documentation:
Consider creating a legacy letter or an ethical will that expresses your principles, life lessons, and goals for future generations.

Support educational activities, such as scholarships or educational programs, to provide others with information and possibilities.

5. Seek Professional Advice
Consult with experts in legacy planning and charity, such as estate planning attorneys and financial consultants. They can assist you in navigating complicated legal and financial issues.

6. Evaluate and Adjust
As circumstances change, assess and adjust your legacy plan on a regular basis. This ensures that your legacy is consistent with your values and ambitions.

Common Mistakes in Legacy Planning
While legacy planning is an admirable goal, there are several common mistakes to avoid:

Procrastination:
Delaying legacy planning might result in wasted opportunities to shape your legacy and ensure your desires are carried out.

Lack of Clarity:
Failure to express your principles and aims might lead to unfocused or inefficient giving.

When incorporating heirs in philanthropic decisions, keep in mind family dynamics and potential conflicts.

Neglecting Professional Advice: Legacy planning frequently entails complex legal and financial issues. Seek the advice of professionals.

Overlooking Tax ramifications:
To maximize the impact of your charity activity and estate plan, be aware of the tax ramifications.

A Legacy of Impact and Influence

Financial independence is a wonderful goal, but it is only the beginning of your financial journey. As you approach this milestone, it's critical to turn your emphasis to leaving a lasting legacy—one that lasts beyond your lifetime and continues to impact the world and those you care about.

Building a legacy is a very personal and purpose-driven activity. It entails identifying your values, making specific goals, and taking purposeful activities to make a positive and lasting influence. Whether your legacy is manifested through financial gifts, knowledge sharing, supporting causes, or sustaining family traditions, it is a monument to wealth's enduring potential to bring about good in the world.

Remember that your legacy is a reflection of your values, passions, and desire to leave the world a better place as you journey from financial independence to legacy creation. It is a gift to future generations, embodying benevolence, charity, and social conscientiousness. Accept the opportunity to leave a legacy that reflects the best of who you are and what you stand for, and you will leave a lasting impact on the world

Conclusion

Conclusion

Dr. Bob Kenneth's "A1 Wealth building: Navigating the Path to Financial Prosperity" has taken us on a revolutionary trip into the complex realm of wealth building. From the start, it was clear that this book would be more than just another financial handbook. It aimed to present readers with not only a road map to wealth, but also a thorough comprehension of the ideas and attitude required to effectively traverse the path to financial prosperity.

As we near the end of this illuminating journey, it is critical that we reflect on the great teachings and insights that Dr. Bob Kenneth has provided with us. This book is more than just a collection of financial advice and strategies; it's a plan for creating a future of financial prosperity and security.

Dr. Kenneth illuminates the way to financial wealth with clarity and wisdom across the pages of "A1 Wealth Creation." He highlighted that true prosperity entails far more than material belongings; it includes financial freedom, peace of mind, and the ability to live life on your own terms. The book walked us through the process of setting meaningful financial objectives, making a good budget, and developing the habit of methodical saving. These fundamental actions form the foundation for financial success.

The necessity of financial education is a reoccurring issue that runs throughout the book. Dr. Kenneth correctly emphasizes that information is power in today's quickly changing financial market. Financial literacy enables people to make informed decisions, negotiate complex investment opportunities, and safeguard their financial future. The book urges readers to be lifelong learners, always looking for new ways to improve their financial knowledge.

Furthermore, "A1 Wealth Creation" emphasizes the importance of thinking in obtaining financial success. Dr. Kenneth deftly delves into the psychology of riches, pushing readers to establish a positive relationship with money. Dispelling limiting notions and cultivating a growth-oriented mentality are critical to realizing one's full financial potential. The book's real-life success tales serve as motivational examples of what is possible with the correct mindset.

The book also underlines the need of risk management in wealth building. While calculated risks are a part of any financial journey, "A1 Wealth Creation" gives a complete roadmap to preserving one's financial well-being. It investigates the significance of insurance, the establishment of emergency funds, and the prudence of diversification. These tactics provide a safety net, ensuring that unanticipated setbacks do not derail your path to prosperity.

Dr. Kenneth pushes for a comprehensive and diversified approach to investing. The book warns against pursuing fads and risky investments, instead advocating for the development of a well-balanced and long-term investing portfolio. It provides excellent insights into numerous investment vehicles, from stocks and bonds to real estate and entrepreneurial initiatives, giving readers the skills they need to make informed decisions that are aligned with their specific financial goals.

Furthermore, "A1 Wealth Creation" dives into the concept of passive income as a means of achieving financial freedom. Dr. Kenneth investigates numerous techniques for establishing recurring money streams, such as dividend investing, rental income, and web enterprises. These passive income streams can progressively diminish your dependency on regular employment income, providing newfound freedom and flexibility.

As we conclude "A1 Wealth Creation: Navigating the Path to Financial Prosperity," keep in mind that your path to financial success is as unique as you are. This book has served as a guidepost, providing concepts and tactics that can be adjusted to your own journey.

To summarize, the actual measure of wealth creation success goes beyond the accumulation of riches; it is found in the beneficial impact it may have on your life and the lives of others. Remember that financial wealth is a means to an end—a means to live a life of purpose, generosity, and fulfillment.

Finally, I encourage you to embark on this adventure with unflinching dedication and enthusiasm. Dr. Bob Kenneth's

"A1 Wealth Creation" has given you the knowledge and wisdom to successfully traverse the route to financial prosperity. Your financial fate is in your control, and equipped with the ideas contained in this book, you are well-prepared to acquire the riches, plenty, and financial freedom you seek. May your path be filled with success, wisdom, and the realization of your dreams.

www.ingramcontent.com/pod-product-compliance
Lightning Source LLC
Chambersburg PA
CBHW062316290526
45794CB00005B/1819